Dear reader

Thank you for investing in this book. I hope that in some small way it will change how you think about and carry out your work.

I'm *deeply* passionate about teacher improvement and determined to make Motivated Teaching a useful contribution to the profession.

If you have suggestions for how I can make this book better, be it a challenge to my arguments or an apostrophe gone astray, please do get in touch – I'd love to hear from you.

Peps
pepsmccrea@gmail.com

About Peps

Peps Mccrea is an award-winning teacher educator, designer and author.

He is Dean of Learning Design at Ambition Institute and holds fellowship awards from the Young Academy and University of Brighton.

Peps has three Masters degrees, two lovely kids, and multiple distracting tattoos (which he'll tell you about over a beer).

Visit **pepsmccrea.com** for the full shebang.

The series

Praise for the *High Impact Teaching* series:

"If you have a spare half-hour or so, you could read *Memorable Teaching* from cover to cover. I doubt you'll find an education book with more useful insights per minute of reading time."
Dylan Wiliam, Emeritus Professor of Educational Assessment at UCL

"How to improve your teaching by planning better. Things that make teachers' lives simpler like that are few and far between."
Doug Lemov, Author of Teach Like a Champion

Motivated Teaching:
Harnessing the science of motivation
to boost attention and effort
in the classroom.

Copyright © 2020 Peps Mccrea
Version 1.2, released November 2020
ISBN 978-1717367204

To Em, for keeping me warm.

Contents*

	Why motivation?	7
	The mechanics of motivation	17
	Motivation for learning	29

The 5 drivers

1.	Secure success	43
2.	Run routines	57
3.	Nudge norms	71
4.	Build belonging	85
5.	Boost buy-in	95

	Pulling it all together	107
	Coda: Motivating ourselves	117
	Thank yous	

---

* For downloadable diagrams and direct links to further readings, visit **pepsmccrea.com/motivation**

Why motivation?

> "Education is mandatory,
> but learning is not."
> Mary Kennedy

Motivation matters. Especially in school.

When pupils are motivated, they pay more attention, put in more effort, persist for longer, and are able to work more independently[1].

Motivated pupils bring *care* and *commitment* to the classroom. When combined with effective curriculum and instruction, they learn more and are a delight to teach.

When pupils *lack* motivation, they get distracted easily, do the bare minimum, require constant cajoling to stay on task, and retain little of what they learn.

Unmotivated pupils bring *apathy* and *avoidance* to the classroom. As a result, they often make slow progress and can be wearingly *hard work* to teach.

Motivation influences the behaviour, learning and life chances of our pupils. Further, it affects the satisfaction and wellbeing of teachers. It is something we should be striving to influence.

Key idea *Motivation influences behaviour, learning and wellbeing*

Not cracked yet

Motivation matters. However, it is not something we have cracked as a profession yet. It is not something we have a sufficiently strong and stable influence on. *Yet.*

Currently, levels of motivation vary widely within the system. At any one time, most schools have some pupils who are *highly motivated*, some who are *not motivated at all*, and many who would benefit from being *even more motivated*.

In addition to widespread variation, there is compelling evidence to suggest that for the average child, levels of motivation *inexorably decline* during compulsory education[2]. Our pupils are leaving school with less drive than when they started.

Motivation for learning may be something we have not yet mastered, but this situation is not for want of trying. Teachers are some of the most dedicated professionals on the planet.

The reason we don't yet have a sufficiently strong and stable influence on motivation is because we don't yet have a sufficiently common and coherent understanding of *what it is* or *how it works*.

The root cause of our struggle to motivate is not a *lack of commitment*, but a *lack of clarity*.

Clarity doesn't come easily

Motivation is something we should be striving to influence. However, it is not something that is easy to understand.

The machinery of motivation evolved over millennia[3], to help us survive and succeed in a world where resources were routinely scarce, competition and collaboration were a constant trade-off, and the outcomes of our actions were often uncertain.

As a consequence of these conditions, the mechanics of motivation are *highly complex*.

Furthermore, this machinery is nested *deep* in our brains and biology. It acts not just in our synapses, but in our genes and in our hormones. It is hard to isolate and often beyond the reach of our conscious awareness.

The mechanics of our motivation are not only *highly complex*, they are also *largely invisible*.

Key idea *Motivation is complex and invisible which makes it hard to understand*

With this in mind, it is little surprise that clarity about motivation doesn't come easily. We can't just open up some heads and look inside, 'trial and error' is insufficient for accurate insight, and introspection alone doesn't have the raw materials to yield enlightenment.

If we truly want to *understand* and *influence* motivation, we've got to look beyond our own experience. We need to look to the *science of motivation*[4].

Even then, clarity still doesn't come easily. The knowledge we need is strewn across multiple fields, plagued by overlapping theories[5] and crises of replication. Frankly, it's a bit of a mess[6].

To gain any kind of actionable clarity from the science, we first need to *tame this mess*.

We need to tease out the most powerful insights that persist *across* fields, codify them in ways we can talk about in the staffroom, and translate them into practices we can deploy with Year 9 on a hot Friday afternoon.

Without this, motivation will forever remain a mystery for schools. An elusive art that some teachers serendipitously develop, but many don't. And the potential of our impact will remain limited.

However, if we *can* achieve this, if we *can harness and tame the science*, we will begin to demystify motivation for schools[7]. We will begin to turn it into a discipline that *all* teachers can master. And ultimately, we will begin to increase our impact.

Which is exactly what this book sets out to do.

Key idea   *To influence motivation, we must draw on insights from science*

Motivated teaching

This book is the result of many years spent studying and attempting to tame the *science of motivation*, alongside my practical experience of helping thousands of teachers and school leaders to improve their game.

It stitches together the best available evidence from multiple fields into a coherent framework that can be harnessed to boost attention and effort in the classroom.

However, what I am offering is neither a quick fix, nor a complete solution. The work of teaching is complex. Changing practice takes time and sustained effort. And motivation is only *one* part of what it takes to be an effective teacher.

If we *really* want to dial up our impact, we must also ensure our pupils have access to great instruction, powerful curricula, and a robust school-wide behaviour system.

It is with these caveats in mind that we begin our journey towards understanding and influence.

The main chapters of this book are organised around 5 'core drivers' of motivation. But before we get there, we first need to make sure we have a clear and common understanding of *what motivation is* and *how it works*.

If you've read my other books, you'll know the score. I've kept things *ultra-concise*, been restrained in my use of examples, and included plenty of links to further reading so you can delve deeper where you want to know more.

It's time to crack on. Grab your highlighter and get ready to dive into *the mechanics of motivation*.

Summary of key ideas

- Motivation influences behaviour, learning and wellbeing
- It is complex and invisible which makes it hard to understand
- To influence motivation, we must draw on insights from science

Notes & further reading

1. For an accessible overview of the range of effects of motivation, see *The crucial role of motivation and emotion in classroom learning* by Boekaerts bit.ly/mot-boe and for some more recent empirical evidence, see Kriegbaum's meta-analysis *The relative importance of motivation in the school context* by https://bit.ly/mot-kri or *Driven to succeed? Teenagers' drive, ambition and performance on high-stakes examinations* by Jerrim bit.ly/mot-jer
2. For example, see *Motivational goals during adolescence* by Mansfield bit.ly/mot-man
3. For a robust overview of evolutionary influences, see *Evolution of the learning brain* by Howard-Jones
4. For more, see *The science of motivation* by Murayama https://bit.ly/mot-mur
5. For more, see *Motivation to learn: an overview of theories* by Cook bit.ly/mot-coo
6. For an account of this 'mess' and how we might fix it, see *Science Fictions* by Richie
7. For some further de-mystification, see *Social-psychological interventions in education: they're not magic* by Yeager bit.ly/mot-yea

Why motivation?

16 Motivated Teaching

The mechanics of motivation

"You can't change what you don't understand."
Scott Card

If we want to influence motivation, we've first got to understand it. To do this properly, we need to take a step back and start with one of the most fundamental aspects of education: *attention*.

Attention is the gatekeeper of learning. *What we attend to is ultimately what we learn*[1].

However, our attention is limited. Like all humans, our pupils can only really attend to one thing at a time. This cognitive constraint has big implications for teaching.

Classrooms can be busy places for the mind. At any given moment, our pupils face acute competition for their attention. From the teacher's voice to the writing on the board. From the *spider in the corner* to someone's *new shoes*.

When faced with these competing opportunities, our pupils must have some way of determining *where* to allocate their limited attention. This is where motivation comes in.

Motivation is the mental system that sifts through the opportunities available to us and determines which we should attend to[2].

Key idea *Motivation is a system for allocating attention*

This is a potent way of thinking about motivation, particularly in school. Not only does it make motivation immediately more *tangible*, but it also tethers it directly to learning, because: *what we are motivated towards is what we attend to*, and *what we attend to is what we learn*.

This definition *also* helps crystallise the critical role of curriculum and instruction in school. Our pupils may be highly motivated, but if we aren't helping them attend to the *right things at the right times*, little learning will occur.

Motivation by itself is insufficient. To fully catalyse learning, we need to think at least as hard about *what we teach* and *how we teach it*.

An investment engine

How does our motivation system determine where to allocate our attention? At the most fundamental level, it appraises the opportunities available to us and predicts which will lead to the greatest *return on investment*[3].

Return on investment is a compound concept. It is the result of three interacting components:

- **Value** What the benefits might be if we invest our attention here, both to us as an individual and to our groups[4].

- **Expectancy** If we *do* invest, the chances of us attaining these benefits.
- **Cost** How much attention and effort we would need to put in.

The opportunity that offers the *greatest value*, *highest expectancy* and *lowest cost* is the one that our attention will be most attracted towards.

At its heart, our motivation system is an *investment engine*, constantly placing bets on where best to allocate our precious attention.

Key idea   *Motivation allocates attention based on the best available investment*

The result of this process doesn't just determine *where* we allocate attention, but also *how much* we should invest. Motivation governs both our *initial choice* and *ongoing effort*.

This is why things like resilience and grit are best thought of as *by-products* of motivation[5]. The more motivated we are towards something, the more persistent we will be in pursuing it.

A largely unconscious process

Our motivation system may be a form of investment engine. However, that doesn't mean we function like a financial spreadsheet, consciously calculating the value, cost and expectancy of every opportunity we face.

There are simply too many opportunities to process at any one time, many of which are intractably complex and continually changing.

Just imagine a pupil trying to work out the best course of action at every crossroads they faced:

Should I pay attention to the teacher? What will happen as a result? To me, and those I care about? Both now, and in the future? What will others think of me for doing so? How will that affect my future? Ad infinitum…

The cognitive demands of *just making a decision* would end up consuming all their attention, leaving little left to invest in the opportunity itself.

Any motivation system that attempted to *consciously reason* through every decision we faced would completely immobilise us. Life is just too great to be contained by the conscious mind.

As a result, we use conscious reasoning sparingly. And for the rest of our decisions (of which there are a *lot*), our motivation system defers to more *unconscious processing*[6].

Key idea *Motivation is a largely unconscious process*

Heuristics

To deal with such abundance and complexity of opportunity, our unconscious often employs 'decision shortcuts'. These 'rules of thumb' are more formally known as *heuristics*[7].

For example, instead of considering *every* variable in calculating our chances of success, we might simply defer to our prior success rate: *how has this kind of task worked out for me before?*

Often these shortcuts lean on our social context. For example, where the value of an opportunity is not clear, we might just look at whether the people around us are doing it: *everyone else seems to be cracking on with the task, so...*

Our heuristics have been honed over millennia to enable us to make *rapid decisions* that lead to *good enough* results across a wide range of situations.

They enable us to survive and thrive in our complex world, but their thrifty nature can mean that different people can easily come to different conclusions about where best to invest their attention.

For some pupils, this will result in listening to the teacher explaining about World War I. For others, it will lead to gazing at a fellow pupil walking by the window.

Fuelled by emotion

Our heuristics are often *fuelled by emotion*[8]. This refers to how our body chemistry and mental circuitry influence our decisions, rather than what we 'feel' (although this can be connected) or what we display to others.

Emotion is such a powerful force that it can often override decisions we arrive at more deliberately, putting us in the strange position of doing things we *wouldn't have consciously chosen to do*.

This internal tension is the basis of our love-hate relationship with chocolate, our uneasy accord with social media, and our variable success with New Year's resolutions.

It's also why *reasoning* with our pupils about their attention will never be a sufficiently reliable strategy by itself. Particularly, if our suggestion is at odds with what their emotional mechanics are telling them.

Regardless of how strong the logic of your pep talk is, few pupils will *ask more questions in class* if they sense it will result in being mocked by their mates.

A fair price

As a profession, we place enormous value on the place of conscious reasoning, and rightly so. It is the backbone of education and has enabled our species to rise above the less civilised aspects of our nature and carve our own moral compass.

It is understandable that we might be wary of the premise that much of our attention and action is subject to highly automatic, emotional processes.

However, without this, we would simply not have the capacity to think more deliberately when desired.

Unconscious processing is a fair price to pay for the ability to learn, be critical and perhaps above all else: be human[9].

If we *really* want to influence attention and effort, then we've got to take an approach that adequately reflects the unconscious dynamics of motivation.

Summary of key ideas

- Motivation is a system for allocating attention
- It allocates attention based on the best available investment
- This is a largely unconscious process

Notes & further reading

1. This was the central thesis of my previous book, *Memorable Teaching*. I'd strongly recommend reading it alongside this one.
2. For more on the crucial link between attention and motivation, see *Cognitive load as motivational cost* by Feldon bit.ly/mot-fel or *The Unified Learning Model* by Shell
3. This 'investment' approach is captured well in the *Expectancy-value-cost model* by Barron bit.ly/mot-bar

4. If you really want to dive into the rabbit hole of inclusive fitness, start with *The inclusive fitness controversy: finding a way forward* by Birch bit.ly/mot-bir
5. For example, see *What shall we do about grit?* By Crede bit.ly/mot-cre
6. This is what Kahneman calls 'System 1' thinking. For more, read his epic *Thinking, fast and slow* or this shorter *Of 2 minds* bit.ly/mot-kah2
7. Heuristics are super interesting! To dip your toe in, see *A fast-and-frugal heuristics approach to performance science* by Raab bit.ly/mot-raa
8. For more, see *Evolving concepts of emotion and motivation* by Berridge bit.ly/mot-ber
9. The interplay between conscious and unconscious processing is fascinating and not quite as clear cut as often implied. Jump into the debate with *Decision science: a new hope* by Curley bit.ly/mot-cur or *Deep Rationality: the evolutionary economics of decision making* by Kenrick bit.ly/mot-ken

Motivation for learning

> "What we still lack is the translation of all this theory into scalable models for practice."
> Rob Coe

One of the most important implications of the previous chapter is that motivation is a *specific response* to the opportunities we face, rather than a *general character trait*[1] of the person we are.

A pupil who is not motivated to learn maths might be highly motivated to play Minecraft. And even this is likely to change depending on the context they are in and the goals they have at the time.

This is why it is unhelpful and inaccurate to talk about Pupil X simply being *motivated or not*.

Instead, it is more productive to talk about Pupil X being *motivated towards something, because of something, in a particular time and place.*

Key idea *Motivation is a specific response to the situation, not a general trait*

This *situation-specificity* is why motivational posters and inspirational quotes rarely achieve lasting impact.

They target a wholesale change in motivation, which might make pupils feel more energised in an assembly but is unlikely to find much purchase when faced with learning about Forces on a Friday afternoon.

Thinking about motivation as a specific response rather than a general trait is an important nuance for schools.

It is *empowering*, because the attractiveness of an opportunity is easier to change than the personality of a pupil.

But it is also *sobering*, because the attractiveness of the opportunities we offer pupils can often be easily undermined by the very nature of school itself.

Not a given

Today's children are expected to learn things that took humankind millennia of accumulated endeavour to understand[2].

Not only is the stuff we teach in school inherently effortful to learn, but its value is not always obvious or immediate. Left to our own devices, few of us would find ourselves with the motivation required to learn such things in full[3].

Even where pupils *do* arrive at school with a natural curiosity, unless we pull the right levers, motivation for learning can easily take a downward trajectory.

Left unchecked, this can lead to pupils graduating with a sense of apathy (or even disdain) toward some subjects, despite having spent multiple years engaging with them.

At best, this is a massive missed opportunity. At worst, it is a travesty of youth.

Motivation for the things we teach is not something we should expect our pupils to walk into school with.

Instead, variable drive is something we must anticipate, take responsibility for, and turn up ready to tackle. As teachers, we must take a *persistently proactive* approach to building motivation for learning.

Key idea *Motivation for learning is something we must actively build*

The core drivers

If we *really* want to turn the dial on motivation for learning, then we need to influence how our pupils appraise the opportunities we offer them.

To achieve this, we must manage the experiences and environment that our pupils encounter in school in ways that harness the systematic nature of their heuristics (decision shortcuts).

There are various ways we can influence pupil attention and effort. Over the coming chapters we will explore the most powerful approaches.

These are the *5 core drivers* (see **next page**), and together with the *key ideas* explored in these opening chapters, they make up the *motivation for learning* framework.

The first two drivers, **success** and **routines**, are heavily economic in nature. They are about how our pupils appraise the value, expectancy and cost of the opportunities we offer[4].

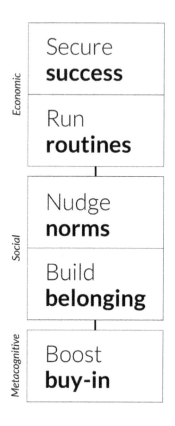

The 5 core drivers of *motivation for learning*

The next two drivers, **norms** and **belonging**, are more social in nature. They are about how the attitudes and actions of others influence our economic appraisal[5].

The final driver, **buy-in**, is metacognitive in nature. It is about how we can cater for preferences of autonomy within the structured context of school.

Together, these drivers provide a framework for action that all teachers can use to build motivation for learning. They take the best available theory and translate it into a *scalable model for practice*.

Key idea *We can systematically build motivation by applying the 5 drivers*

The next five chapters of this book each explore one core driver in detail. After this, we take a chapter to pull them all together, before ending with another on how we might apply the framework to *ourselves*.

Fun & rewards

There are two common strategies that are notably absent in the framework:

- **Making lessons fun** Such as designing a lesson around football to lure the fanatics.
- **Offering simple rewards** Such as sweets or stickers for those who work the hardest.

Fun is an important part of life, and the above approaches *can* sometimes motivate. However, they are not part of the framework because they attract attention towards the *fun* or *reward itself*, rather than the learning opportunity at hand.

In short, they are *extrinsic* rather than *intrinsic* drivers[6].

With extrinsic drivers, we can easily find ourselves with pupils who have thought more about football than phonemes. They are simply not effective strategies for building long-term motivation for learning.

At best, extrinsic drivers have a *fleeting* impact. Just as when we stretch an elastic band, motivation just returns to prior levels once these external forces are removed.

At worst, they can have a *detrimental* impact. Just as paying people to give blood can signal that the task is undesirable, they can leave motivation at even lower levels than before.

Where we *do* employ the temporary scaffolds of extrinsic drivers, we should use them *as little as possible*, and remove them *as soon as we can*[7].

In contrast, the principles and strategies outlined in the following chapters are *intrinsic drivers*. Implemented effectively, they will attract attention towards the learning opportunity itself.

As such, they should be used *as much as possible*, and kept in place *as long as we can*.

Effective implementation

The 5 drivers are not a sequence. They don't have to be deployed in order. However, they *are* additive. The more that are active at any given moment, the stronger the effect will be.

Whilst it has been designed primarily to *catalyse* motivation, the 5 core drivers can also be used to *inhibit* it. For example, to reduce the attention a pupil is paying towards something distracting, we can simply reverse the polarity: *decrease expectancy, increase cost, reduce belonging etc.*

Either way, it is important to recognise that *Motivated Teaching* is a long-term approach. Anticipated changes will likely take time to emerge and be modest to begin with[8].

Furthermore, the highly social nature of human behaviour means that the actions of colleagues and the broader culture of school will have a persistent effect on how things pan out in your classroom.

This is why building motivation is best done collectively. Every colleague that is in alignment multiplies the benefit for both you and your pupils (and them and their pupils).

So *do* share the ideas in this book. But just take care how you do it. Without a secure understanding of the key ideas and nuances, we risk developing 'lethal' mutations: practices that can do more harm than good[9].

The tools outlined in *Motivated Teaching* increase our potential *power* in the classroom. As with any tool, they can be used for various ends, some more benign than others.

More than ever, we must exercise our moral judgement as teachers. True professionalism requires us to put ethics at its heart[10].

But professional judgement also requires knowledge. And so, without further ado, let's get stuck into the core drivers.

Summary of key ideas

- Motivation is a specific response to the situation, not a general trait
- *Motivation for learning* is something we must actively build
- We can systematically build it by applying the 5 drivers

Notes & further reading

1. Unhelpfully, we often have a tendency to assume the opposite. This cognitive bias is known as 'Fundamental Attribution Error' or 'Correspondence Bias'
2. Thinking about education through this lens is mind-blowing. See *How culture makes us smarter* by Stewart-Williams bit.ly/mot-ste
3. For possible explanations, see *Conditions for intuitive expertise* (the 'low validity environment' argument) by Kahneman bit.ly/mot-kah and *Educating the evolved mind* (the 'biologically secondary' argument) by Geary bit.ly/mot-gea
4. The theory that aligns closest here is the *Expectancy-value-cost model of motivation* by Barron bit.ly/mot-bar

5. The theory that aligns closest here is *Self-determination theory* by Ryan bit.ly/mot-rya
6. See *The emerging neuroscience of intrinsic motivation* by Domenico bit.ly/mot-dom > however, the distinction between intrinsic and extrinsic motivation is probably smaller and more subtle than tends to be claimed > for more, see *Revisiting the role of rewards in motivation and learning* by Hidi bit.ly/mot-hid
7. For a great overview of the evidence around rewards, see *Should learning be its own reward?* by Willingham bit.ly/mot-wil2 and for some insight on the neurological mechanics under all this, see *A neuroscientific view on classroom motivation* by Hobbiss bit.ly/mot-hob
8. For further nuance on implementation, see *Nudging in education* by Damgaard bit.ly/mot-dam or *Addressing achievement gaps with psychological interventions* by Yeager bit.ly/mot-yea2
9. For a great primer, see *Avoiding 'lethal mutations'* by Rose bit.ly/mot-ros
10. For an exploration of the ethics of influence in school, see *Is nudging OK?* by Fletcher-Wood bit.ly/mot-fle3

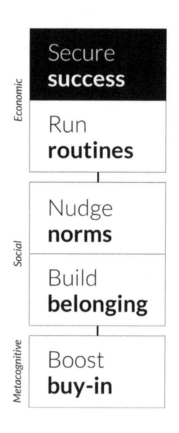

1

Secure **success**

> "Good teachers have this ability to get pupils to care about stuff they didn't care about when they walked into the classroom."
> Dylan Wiliam

Our motivation is heavily influenced by our anticipation of future success: the likelihood that we will reap the benefits, for ourselves or for our groups, if we invest in an opportunity. This likelihood gauge is known as *expectancy*[1].

It makes sense to have evolved a gauge like this. With such limited attention to allocate, it would be crazy to invest heavily in opportunities that are unlikely to bear fruit.

Expectancy is heavily shaped by prior success rate. The more successful we have been in the past, the more likely we are to invest in similar opportunities in the future.

Pupils who experience high levels of success in the classroom tend to tackle more challenging problems, organise their ideas better, and see things from a greater number of perspectives[2].

Expectancy is fragile

Expectancy is one of the most potent enablers of learning. But it is also one of the most fragile.

The things we teach are hard to learn, and the steady march through curricula in schools can be unrelenting. The risk of failure for pupils is ever present, and the costs associated with it can be high: anxiety, damage to ego, loss of status.

Without a firm conviction that success is likely, initial effort can quickly wane and be replaced with apathy, and eventually, avoidance.

Over time, repeated failure can lead to deep-seated beliefs, such as: *I can't do this, I'm no good at Spanish*, and *there's no point*. Left unchecked, these beliefs can unfold into self-fulfilling prophecies and erect barriers to future learning.

Those of us who have taught pupils with these kinds of beliefs know just how destructive they can be. The costs of low expectancy can be catastrophic and stubbornly hard to reverse.

If we want to maximise motivation for learning, we must take a deliberate approach to *securing success*.

Just great teaching

Securing success is *not* about making things easier for pupils. It is about helping them do something they couldn't do before.

As a rough rule of thumb, we want pupils to be able to look back on an average success rate of at least 80%[3]. Ways to achieve this include:

- **Precise pitching** Provide learning experiences that are challenging yet achievable for as many pupils as possible.
- **Granular chunking** Breaking ideas and processes down so they can be learned in small parts before being built back up.

Of course, it also helps if you also explain things clearly and provide feedback to keep your class on track. In short, expectancy (and therefore motivation) is in no small part the result of *just great teaching*.

Framing success

One of the challenges of fostering widespread expectancy is the *subjective nature of success*. Our past experiences are filtered through a lens of meaning. One pupil's success can easily be another pupil's failure.

Regardless of how well we teach, some pupils may still interpret their experience as a failure. And so, to fully lock in success, we also need to *frame it*[4]. Ways to achieve this include:

- **Get there first** Don't leave success open to interpretation: define it before your pupils do. Provide examples of *what it looks like*, and *what it doesn't*. Call it when you see it.
- **Use the right metric** Feedback on the learning behind the performance. Talk about what they *know* or are *able to do*, rather than their progress on a task.
- **Self-reference** Frame pupil progress against their *own* past performances, rather than those of their peers.

As well as framing success, we can also attempt to *directly* influence perceptions of expectancy. For example, by repeatedly messaging, through both our talk and action, that *I believe you can*[5].

However, we must be careful not to *over-promise*. Telling a pupil: *you're good at maths* or *you can do it* is unlikely to stand for long in the face of contrary experience. Promises of success that don't eventually materialise will only serve to undermine motivation and erode trust.

Accurate attribution

Expectancy is not just influenced by how we interpret our performance, but also what we perceive to be the *cause* of that performance[6].

Only where pupils believe they were successful *and* they attribute the cause to themselves – *their own effort, ability and approach* – will their expectancy increase.

Where they believe success is the result of external factors – *an unfair test, a biased teacher, or just plain bad (or good) luck* – their expectancy will remain unchanged.

A worst-case scenario arises when pupils attribute failure to *themselves* – their effort, ability and approach – and believe these things to be *beyond their control*.

To maximise expectancy, we must help our pupils understand that failure can be changed, and success can be sustained. We must help them develop *accurate attribution*.

To help achieve this, we can:

- **Stabilise the environment** Provide learning experiences that put pupils in control of their outcomes. Reduce the influence of external factors and, where possible, provide objective measures of success.
- **Assign attributions** Regularly point out the causes of pupil success and failure. Help them to see how effort and approach can make a difference.
- **Spotlight improvement** Look back at progress over time to prove to pupils that their proficiency is malleable, and something they can directly influence.

Mitigating failure

Expectancy is more easily destroyed than developed and is at its most vulnerable in the initial stages of learning. With only a few experiences to draw upon, each early success or failure can have an inordinate effect on pupil motivation.

However, despite our efforts, pupils will fail. It is an inevitable part of school, and probably an important lesson for life.

And so, during these early experiences, not only do we want to be deliberate in our efforts to secure success, we also want to put in place steps to *mitigate failure*. To do this, we can:

- **Pre-empt** Communicate that failure is a natural and expected part of school and life. That it has happened before and that people, like them, have bounced back.
- **Reframe** Celebrate failure as an opportunity to learn[7]. This can also compensate for the inevitable negative (and potentially cognitively impairing) emotions that accompany failure. Move on quickly or 'restart' as required.
- **Reattribute** Message that if pupils *are* following guidance and putting in the effort, then it is more likely a *failure of the system*. For example, of the teacher not pitching or chunking well enough.

The power of proficiency

Over time, if we get the level of challenge right, repeated success doesn't just increase *expectancy*, it also generates *proficiency*.

Proficiency is obviously a desirable outcome, being a core goal of education. However, it is also advantageous from a motivational perspective, because it boosts the perceived *value* of an opportunity. It does this by fostering:

- **Agency** The more we know, the greater our sense of power to act in the world.
- **Curiosity** The more we know, the more gaps in understanding we strive to fill[8].
- **Awe** The more we know, the more wondrous the world becomes.
- **Fluency** Being able to do things quickly and accurately is simply a satisfying feeling.
- **Sunk cost** Getting increasingly proficient means this thing must be a worthwhile investment, right?

The more proficient we get, the more our perception of value increases, and the more we invest in similar opportunities. When success generates proficiency, motivation becomes as much a *product* of learning as it is the *driver* of it[9].

Catalysing this reciprocal relationship is the *compound interest* of great teaching, and the most sustainable approach to forging enduring motivation.

And so, if we care about building motivation for the long run, we must *prioritise proficiency*. It is the ultimate self-fuelling engine of education.

Scholarly identity

Repeated success generates expectancy at increasingly 'deeper' levels. As this happens, we construct narratives to explain and give meaning to these recurring emotional experiences.

Over time, pupils can move from telling themselves that *I can do these questions* to *I can do fractions* to *I am good at maths*. Eventually, if this is replicated across subjects, some may even get to the point of thinking *I am a great learner*[10].

As pupil expectancy deepens, their tolerance for challenge and failure grows, and their perceptions of success become more nuanced. Over time, we can push them harder and worry less about maintaining a consistent success rate.

Getting to this point can take years of collaborative endeavour. However, it's totally worth it. Setting pupils up as committed *life-long learners* is one of the greatest gifts we can give.

Summary of core strategies

- Give your pupils a high success rate to look back on
- Frame what success means and help them attribute it accurately
- Pre-empt failure

Notes & further reading

1. Also known as 'self-efficacy'
2. For more on benefits and detriments, see *The crucial role of motivation and emotion in classroom learning* by Boekaerts bit.ly/mot-boe or *Revisiting the role of rewards in motivation & learning* by Hidi bit.ly/mot-hid
3. Rosenshine popularised this '80% rule' in *Principles of instruction* bit.ly/mot-ros2
4. For even more strategies, see *Nudging in education* by Damgaard bit.ly/mot-dam
5. For more nuance here, see *Teacher expectations and self-fulfilling prophecies* by Jussim bit.ly/mot-jus
6. For more, see *How learning works* by Ambrose bit.ly/mot-amb
7. Lemov has lots of great strategies around 'culture of error' in *Teach Like A Champion*
8. For a nice overview, see *Homo curious: curious or interested* by Shin bit.ly/mot-shi
9. For example, see *Reciprocal effects of self-concept and achievement* by Marsh bit.ly/mot-mar
10. For more on 'academic self-concept', see *The Importance of students' motivation for their academic achievement* by Steinmayr bit.ly/mot-ste2

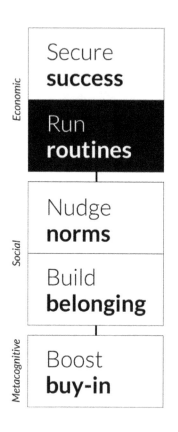

2

Run **routines**

> "Most of the time what we do is what we do most of the time."
> Townsend & Bever

Value and expectancy are important influences on motivation. However, there is one other economic factor that also has a significant sway on our allocation of attention: *cost*[1].

Cost is how much attention and effort we sense we'll have to invest to attain the benefits of an opportunity. The lower the cost, the more motivated we will be[2].

Many people appreciate the benefits of being able to speak a second language and believe this is something they have the capacity to achieve.

However, few end up doing so simply because of the effort required. If we could learn a language in a day, we'd have a much more multilingual society.

If we want to maximise motivation in the classroom, we must think beyond what our pupils will *get out* of a lesson – we must think just as hard about what they need to *put in*.

The economics of learning

In many areas of life, cost can be reduced by simply making the task *easier*. We see this in the rise of one-click purchasing and Deliveroo. When something requires less effort, our *return on investment* appraisal tips, and we find ourselves more compelled to act.

However, reducing *cost* in school is not quite so straightforward. The things we teach are inherently effortful to acquire – they demand sustained attention and the continual construction of meaning. If we made everything easy, little learning would occur.

And so, whilst motivation is catalysed by *less* effort, learning is fuelled by *more*. How do we resolve this knotty pedagogical dilemma?

The answer lies in distinguishing between the *what* and the *how* of learning.

Both contribute to overall pupil effort, but it is possible to reduce the demand generated by the *how* whilst maintaining the exertion generated by the *what*. This entails making the *process* of learning easy, whilst keeping the *content* of learning challenging.

One of the most powerful and sustainable ways to achieve this is by *running routines* in our lessons.

The anatomy of routines

Routines strip out redundant decision costs, reduce the amount of novel information that we have to process, and make the most of our ability to *think less about the things we repeatedly do.*

They hack the attention economy of the classroom to help pupils *learn hard things faster.*

A routine is a sequence of actions triggered by a specific prompt or 'cue' that is repeated so often it becomes an unconscious, automatic response[3]. They are the habit architecture of organisations, the 'if-then' algorithms of life. *If X happens, I do Y.*

School routines fall into two camps:

- **Behavioural routines** These create more time and space for learning. For example, a well-honed classroom entry or exit.
- **Instructional routines** These help pupils make the most of learning opportunities. For example, carefully designed questioning or discussion protocols.

One of the great things about routines is that teachers have been running them since the profession began. Examples abound in the classrooms around us. If we want inspiration, we only need look with the right lens.

There have also been a few attempts to capture and codify effective routines. See *Teach Like A Champion* and *Instructional Activities for the Math(s) Classroom* for great examples of these.

Watching peers and drawing on resources is an efficient way to grow your repertoire of routines. However, there will also be times when you need to *build your own*.

Building bespoke routines requires the careful consideration and construction of two things[4]:

- **A chain** What exactly will your pupils do?
- **A cue** What will start this chain of action?

A *chain* is simply a sequence of actions. We all have loads in our lives already: *Get up > Have breakfast > Brush teeth > Get dressed > Go to work.*

The most effective chains are:

- **Simple** A single chain of actions that flow naturally from one to the next, easily remembered and requiring minimal consideration, decision or support.
- **Clear cut** Where possible, actions should be things that can be considered *done or not done*, rather than *partially done*. This makes it easier for you and your pupils to enact and maintain the routine.
- **Stepped** Making the first action easy helps pupils get off the blocks. This *micro-investment* can also build a sense of commitment to fuel the rest of the routine.

A *cue* is a prompt that kickstarts the first action in the chain. They are executed by a person or simply exist in the environment: *The alarm clock that gets us up. The close of the front door that cues us to put our keys away and kick off our shoes.*

Cues are an oft overlooked aspect of behaviour. But without them, routines won't get off the runway.

The most effective cues are:

- **Distinct** The more unique the cue, the less chance it will be misinterpreted as a prompt for another routine. You don't want your pupils *packing up their bags* every time you raise your hand.
- **Multimodal** Make your cue easily sensed by combining noise or speech with action and position. *Go to a place, perform a gesture, issue an instruction.*
- **Punchy** The 100m starter gun is your idol.

Over time, you can make your cue increasingly subtle. Eventually, complex cascades of action will flow from the mere tilt of an eyebrow.

Routines are often a major ingredient in the social infrastructure of schools. However, they rarely get the intentional design they deserve.

Taking a lens to those aspects of classroom life that regularly repeat can pay dividends in learning over time. Ask yourself: *Which parts of my lesson frequently recur? How might they be better?*

As your repertoire of routines grows, you'll need to pay increasing attention to how they fit together. You may wish to consider:

- **Stacking** Putting routines 'back-to-back' where the end of one is the cue for the start of another.
- **Nesting** Placing routines *within* routines. How grand and how granular can you go?

Where you can, *replace* routines rather than *adding* new ones. This will help keep your lessons streamlined and avoid bloat.

Effective rollouts

Once you've designed your routine, you're ready to start *rolling it out*.

Boost your chances of success by doing this when the conditions are ripe. 'Fresh start' moments such as *after a test* or *the start of a term* often find pupils at their most receptive, and teachers at our most determined[5].

The most effective rollouts are:

- **Explicit** Tell and show your pupils exactly what to do at each step. Don't leave them to (mis)join the dots.
- **Labelled** Make it easier to talk about and refine the routine by giving each step and cue a simple, sticky name.
- **Scaffolded** Make the environment work for you. For example, using alarm clocks, book boxes, or structure strips[6] to make it *easy* for pupils to do the right thing.

Sticking with it

Routines can be powerful tools, but their benefits only really arise once they've become *automated*.

The amount of time it takes for a routine to automate depends on its complexity and how frequently it gets performed. A simple routine can take up to 20 runs to become automatic. More complex procedures can take up to 200[7].

We can accelerate the *time to automation* by:

- **Holding steady** Keep the cue and the chain the same and run the routine every time you need it.
- **Running rehearsals** Practise the routine even when you *don't* need it. This can also be done as a mental walkthrough.

During this *automating phase*, routines can often feel like they are more effort than they're worth. It can be tempting to give up[8].

However, if you *stick with it*, there will come a tipping point where the benefits begin to outweigh the investment. And from then on, your routine will pay back handsomely.

The benefits of routines don't just stop at increased motivation and learning. For many pupils, they can generate increased feelings of safety, confidence and wellbeing. And for teachers, they reduce the behaviour burden, and free up precious mental resources to monitor learning and make teaching more responsive[9].

Summary of key ideas

- Make the *process* of learning easy, whilst keeping the *content* of learning challenging
- Design your own routines by scripting chains and designing cues
- Stick with it

Notes & further reading

1. For more, see *Expectancy-value-cost model* by Barron bit.ly/mot-bar
2. This is one of the foundational tenets of behavioural economics. For a highly readable overview of this and more, see *EAST: Four simple ways to apply behavioural insights* by Service bit.ly/mot-ser
3. For a more comprehensive look at routine building, see *Atomic Habits* by Clear and for a good treatment of this in an educational context, see *Running the room* by Bennett

4. For more, see *The four stages of habit* by Clear bit.ly/mot-cle2 or *Habits for Lifelong Learning: Applying Behavioral Insights to Education* by Gustafson bit.ly/mot-gus > note that I have omitted the 'reward' stage. This is because reward in the classroom is best treated as an intrinsic property of the system, as so fulfilled through the 5 drivers
5. For more, see *Helping students maintain habits* by Fletcher-Wood bit.ly/mot-fle
6. For example, see this *Structure Strips* sutori bit.ly/mot-sut and for endless ideas, just nudge @mrlockyer on twitter
7. For more on habit formation, see *Making health habitual: the psychology of 'habit formation'* by Gardner bit.ly/mot-gar
8. This is known as the 'hot stove effect'. For more, see *Teacher journal clubs: how do they work and how can they increase evidence-based practice* by Sims bit.ly/mot-sim
9. Routines are a cornerstone of teacher expertise. For more, see *Describing the behaviour and documenting the accomplishments of expert teachers* by Berliner bit.ly/mot-ber2

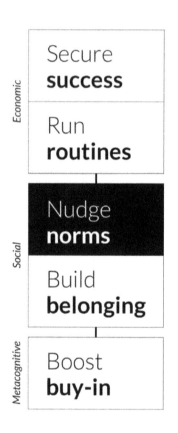

3

Nudge **norms**

> "One dog barks at something, and a hundred bark at the bark."
> Chinese proverb

We are motivated towards opportunities that appear to come with high value, high expectancy and low cost. However, in our complex and dynamic world, these things are not always easy to determine.

As a result, in attempting to figure out where best to allocate our attention, we've evolved to refer heavily to the *behaviour and attitudes of others*[1].

This 'imitation' shortcut makes sense[2]. *If those around us are doing it, it can't be all that bad a bet.*

The effect is particularly powerful when a large proportion of a community acts in a similar way for a given situation. These 'unwritten rules of conduct' are known as *social norms*[3].

A quick and safe bet

As well as being drawn to social norms as a means of investing attention, we are also often pressured into *conforming* to them by our peers.

This is because norms are such an important enabling condition for large group co-operation.

Working together at scale can supercharge our individual and collective success, through mechanisms such as *division of labour* and *economies of scale*. But these things are only possible when the behaviour of individuals within a community is consistent and predictable.

Just imagine trying to watch a film at the cinema or get served at a bar where people didn't take cues about how to behave from others. Without norms, society would be chaos[4].

As a result, we have evolved a tendency not only to *imitate* norms, but to *enforce* them.

Where norms are established, individuals within a group often work together to penalise those who don't conform.

Sanctions can involve the removal of status (with all the benefits it brings), and eventually being *outcast* which, in our ancestral environment, would have significantly hampered our prospects of survival.

Not only does imitating others increase our odds of success, it also reduces our risk. Conforming to social norms is both a *quick* and *safe* bet[5].

Norms in school

Norms play as big a role in school as they do in life, if not more so. They are the reason teachers can get 30 pupils to work diligently on sentence structure for an hour whilst some parents struggle for the same time to get one child to put on a sock [*yes, I'm talking from experience here*].

Norms are so powerful they often override more formal school policies or rules. However, their largely invisible and unconscious nature makes them easy to underestimate, if not totally ignore.

This lack of awareness is the root of much frustration in school. Trying to get your pupils to pay attention where undesirable norms are in place – such as *not asking questions*, *not putting in effort*, or *not aspiring to further education* – can be a futile endeavour.

The *emergence* of norms is inevitable. There is little we can do about it. However, the *nature* of these norms *is* within our influence.

If we want to secure motivation for learning, we must both *acknowledge* and *leverage* the influence of group behaviour on individual action. We need to *nudge norms*.

Elevating visibility

The norms we hold arise predominantly from our observation of others. To modify motivation, we must change what our pupils *see*. We can make desirable norms more *visible* by increasing their:

1. **Profusion** The proportion of pupils that appear to conform to a norm.
2. **Prominence** How visceral and memorable our sightings of norm compliance are.

Increasing *profusion* simply entails pushing for maximum uptake. Getting as many pupils as you can to embrace a desirable behaviour. 100% adoption is the ultimate outcome – the presence of even a single dissenter makes it easier for others not to follow along.

When we see one person picking up litter, doing it ourselves becomes a slightly safer option. When we see *everyone* picking up litter, not doing it ourselves becomes a risk.

Increasing *prominence* entails making desired norms more readily seen and sensational. We can achieve this by pointing out positive behaviour when we see it, telling stories of it happening in other contexts, and even modelling it ourselves[6].

Stories can be powerful tools for shaping culture. They weave, chunk and sequence information in ways that make it more meaningful and memorable[7].

Where we do lean on narrative, it's best to be explicit about the norm we are advocating, articulate the rationale behind it, and include multiple, recent examples.

Where there isn't an *established norm*, we can point to evidence of an *emerging norm*. A behaviour that appears to be growing in adoption and approval.

Or we can point to *norm outcomes*. A full pile of homework books handed in or a tidy classroom when pupils enter are strong signals that *homework gets done around here* and *we keep this classroom tidy*.

Elevating the visibility of norms works best when teachers have a vivid sense of what 'desirable' actually means. To nudge towards norms for impact, we must first gain clarity on *what we want*.

Amplifying approval

Our perception of norms is not just influenced by the *actions* of others, but also their *attitudes*[8]. When a group appears to *approve* of an action, even when they don't *do it*, we will feel the draw of that behaviour.

Approval can be signalled by teachers – *what we permit, we promote*. But it is *much* more powerful when it comes from peers.

Ways to amplify peer approval include:

- **Peer shout-outs** At the end of a lesson, ask your class to identify pupils who have been pushing themselves or supporting others.
- **Ritual recognition** When someone demonstrates a desirable behaviour or attitude, publicly *catch them being good*, and then get the class to give them some finger snaps or a mini-applause.
- **Pass the mic** Periodically ask pupils to *stand and share* how they learned effectively today or overcame an obstacle.

Peer approval is why regular exposure to positive role models can be so powerful. When we see someone we identify with *achieving*, or simply *acting like they believe they can*, this opens up our own possibility space.

Normative nuance

There are several things to be mindful of when nudging norms. Firstly, normative messaging appears to be more effective when it emphasises what we *want to happen*, rather than what we *don't*[9].

Chastising a class by messaging that the majority of them didn't do their homework is more likely to act as a reinforcement rather than a deterrent.

Secondly, normative messaging is most potent in novel situations. This is why it is worth taking time to *get things right* in the early days of establishing a class. Once norms have taken hold, they become increasingly hard to change.

It is also why some schools host new classes for a few days at the start of the year, before the rest of the school begins[10]. It provides the elbowroom needed to get desirable norms and routines established before the rest of the party arrive.

Finally, the social nature of approval means that the norms of different groups within a school will naturally bleed into each other. When these interacting norms *oppose* each other, both attenuate. But when interacting norms *support* each other, both grow stronger.

This is why it can be so powerful to put *North Star norms* at the heart of your whole-school narrative. They give everyone something to look to and line up behind in times of ambiguity.

North Star norms

North Star norms shine brightest when they are simple and actionable: *work hard, aim high, be kind*. And where the whole school community gets behind them: *teachers, peers, parents, alumni, big brothers and sisters...*

Establishing school-wide norms requires an *allegiance to consistency* from all colleagues. This is not always straightforward to achieve, but it's totally worth the endeavour.

Because when colleagues are aligned, not only does pupil motivation become supercharged, but everyone's work life also becomes easier. Which is no small deal for anyone, and a particularly big one for staff new to a school.

Summary of key ideas

- Elevate the visibility of desirable norms
- Amplify peer approval
- Emphasise what you *want* to happen, not what you *don't*

Notes & further reading

1. To the extent that we are hardwired to share attention with others, as suggested by Howard-Jones in *Evolution of the learning brain*. This social mediation of classical economics is the basis of a relatively new field: *behavioural economics*. For a helpful overview, see *An introduction to behavioural economics* by Samson bit.ly/mot-sam
2. This is sometimes referred to as 'Social proof'. For more, see *Social influence: compliance and conformity* by Cialdini bit.ly/mot-cia
3. For more on this fascinating aspect of human behaviour, see *Norm perception as a vehicle for social change* by Tankard bit.ly/mot-tan

4. For an example of a modern 'Asch experiment' (herd mentality), see *Most people are sheep* bit.ly/mot-asc
5. For more, see *Social influence: compliance and conformity* by Cialdini bit.ly/mot-cia and for a school perspective on norms, see *Running the room* by Bennett
6. For further strategies and a great read on behaviour change in general, see *Switch: how to change things when change is hard* by the Heath Brothers
7. For more, see *The privileged status of story* by Willingham bit.ly/mot-wil4
8. For more, see *How learning works* by Ambrose bit.ly/mot-amb
9. For an example, see *How riding the herd mentality may have helped by GCSE classes* by Theo bit.ly/mot-the and for further nuance around the underpinning evidence, see *'Broken windows' theory debunked* by St. Martin bit.ly/mot-stm
10. For an example of this being applied, see *Bootcamp breaks the bad habits* by Kirby bit.ly/mot-kir

Build belonging 83

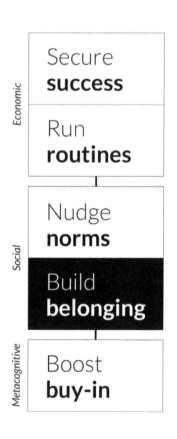

4

Build **belonging**

> "It feels good to learn where I belong."
> Un Fong Lam

Social norms shape our motivation. However, the strength of their influence depends on how much we *feel part of* and *identify with* those exhibiting the norms. Motivation is mediated by *belonging*[1].

The more we feel we belong to a group, the more we invest in its goals and conform to its norms. The less we feel we belong to a group, the less we will be open to its influence, to the extent that we may even *oppose* what it advocates.

Belonging doesn't just drive motivation and learning, it impacts health and happiness too.

Being part of something bigger than ourselves simply *feels good*, whereas *not fitting in* can fuel depression, reduce life expectancy, and even increase the risk of teen suicide[2].

The need for kinship is particularly prevalent in times of personal change. It is little surprise that belonging can be a core concern for many pupils, and potentially *all-consuming* for adolescents.

Even where schools *are* able to build belonging, there can sometimes be undesirable side-effects. Part of what defines a group is not only *who is in* but *who is out*. And this distinction can sometimes be based on superficial characteristics[3].

Left unchecked, grouping within schools can easily divide as much as unite, prejudicing those pupils who stand to *benefit from belonging* the most[4]. For reasons of equity *as much as* motivation, it's important that we take an intentional approach to *building belonging*.

Signalling status

When people come together around a common purpose and take responsibility for contributing, everyone within the group stands to benefit.

'Teaming up' enables the pooling of resources and playing of specialist roles to achieve agreed aims or support members who are struggling. However, the spoils of collective endeavour are typically only shared amongst recognised members of the group.

Status is a signal of our standing within a group. The degree to which our membership is acknowledged, our contribution is appreciated, and our preferences are respected.

At any one time, myriad overlapping social groups will exist in school, most of which we will have limited influence over. However, the collectives we *can* shape are those of our classes.

We can signal status for *everyone* in our classes by:

- **Recognising** Highlighting contributions that individuals make to the group, particularly those on the periphery.
- **Including** Ensuring that everyone is included in class activities, discussions, jokes and celebrations.
- **Framing** Using the language of *we and us* rather than *you and me*, to emphasise the collective nature and shared fate of classroom activity.

How we frame *feedback* is a particularly sensitive area. Pupils can easily interpret feedback as criticism from the teacher and a sign of rejection. *You've got this question incorrect* can easily become *I am not accepted here*.

We can turn this risk into a resource by framing feedback as a defining feature of the group. *In this class, we all push each other, because we care about everyone getting better*[5].

Cultivating affinity

In addition to having status, for belonging to flourish we also need to feel *affinity* with a group.

If status is about 'how much they like me', then affinity is about 'how much they *are* like me'. It is the degree to which we understand and align with the values and perspectives of other members[6].

The more that members of a group identify with each other, the greater their confidence that the collective will *invest in opportunities they approve of* and *generate outcomes they appreciate*. Strategies for cultivating affinity in our classes include[7]:

- **Unifying purpose** Setting a clear agenda for the group, helping them see the benefits and getting everyone lined up behind it. *We're going to nail these exams.*

- **Shared identity** Developing distinctive language, ways of working, or lesson rituals that can act as a common reference point for the class. *Here, we do this.*
- **Common ground** Prompting pupils to look for personal connections in areas such as their background, interests or shared experiences. *Cool, you like Minecraft too!*

The more unique and enduring the connection, the stronger the resulting effect. Finding out that you *speak the same second language* as someone is more affiliating than seeing them *eat the same lunch*.

Cultivating affinity can build belonging *within* a class, but if we're not careful, it can also create divisions *between* classes. We can mitigate this downside by constructing a group identity that actively *respects* those beyond the group.

Even competing with another class can be affiliating if it's done in the right way. Respectful, light-hearted and *sportspersonly* rivalries can create common ground between groups and foster greater *whole-school belonging* for all.

Earning trust

The final piece of the belonging puzzle is *trust*. Working with others requires us to take a leap of faith that they will make decisions and allocate resources fairly on our behalf. The more trust that is present, the more we will feel we belong, and the more attention we will invest.

In school, it is *desirable* for pupils to have faith in their friends, but it is *essential* that they have trust in their teacher.

When trust is present, pupils will readily embrace teacher suggestions about where to allocate their attention and effort. When trust is absent, pupils can view teacher direction as an inconvenience, or even with suspicion, and ultimately reject or undermine it altogether.

As a teacher, status is something you get *bestowed* upon you by the school, whereas trust is something you must *earn* from your pupils. We can earn trust by demonstrating:

- **Credibility** *Is my teacher knowledgeable enough to lead me in the right direction?* Showcase your accomplishments and expertise, in the curriculum and beyond. Get others they trust to vouch for you.
- **Care** *Does my teacher understand and look out for me?* Take visible action to show your pupils that you know them, you are on their side, and you have their interests at heart. As Roosevelt said: "kids don't care what you know until they know that you care."
- **Consistency** *Is my teacher predictable and fair?* Be transparent in your values and expectations. Communicate them regularly and ensure they align with your actions. Exhibit steadfast emotional stability.

Trust takes time to earn and discipline to keep. But as any experienced hand will tell you: *it's worth it*. The classroom is so much more efficient and enjoyable when pupils have confidence in their teacher.

When all three ingredients are in place – *status*, *affinity* and *trust* – belonging will bloom. And in the socially saturated environment of school, the resulting effect on motivation can be profound.

Summary of key ideas

- Signal the status of *all* pupils in your class
- Develop a unifying purpose and identify common ground
- Earn and keep trust

Notes & further reading

1. For more, see *An evolutionary perspective on social identity* by Brewer bit.ly/mot-bre
2. For more on the benefits and detriments, see *Mere belonging: the power of social connections* by Walton bit.ly/mot-wal
3. For more, see *What every teacher needs to know about psychology* by Didau & Rose
4. For more, see *How people learn II: learners, contexts, and cultures* by NAS bit.ly/mot-nat
5. Lemov has lots of great strategies around 'culture of error' in *Teach Like A Champion*
6. For more, see *Creating birds of a similar feathers: leveraging similarity to improve teacher-student relationships and academic achievement* by Gehlbach go.aws/mot-geh
7. For more strategies, see *Nudging in education* by Damgaard bit.ly/mot-dam

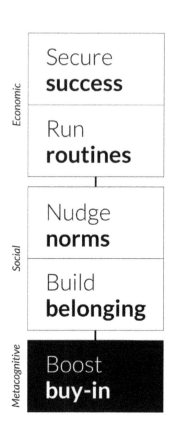

5

Boost **buy-in**

> "We make our decisions,
> and then our decisions make us."
> Frank Boreham

In a world where the behaviours and attitudes of others have such influence over our own, we are attracted towards opportunities that give us a measure of *autonomy* or *choice* over our actions.

However, not all choice is equally motivating. It can be more frustrating than empowering when we have *too many options*, the alternatives are things we *don't care about*, or we feel we are not the best person to make the decision[1]. For choice to be motivating, it must also be *meaningful*.

Where our pupils feel they have meaningful choice, they will put in more effort, persist for longer, and enjoy their learning more[2]. Where our pupils feel they have meaningless choice or are being coerced, they will invest less or even actively resist.

The challenge of choice in school

Offering meaningful choice in the classroom is not straightforward, particularly when it comes to the macro-mechanics of education: *what to learn* and *how to learn it*.

The nature of the things we teach combined with the novice status of our pupils means they simply *don't know what they don't know*.

Just as patients lack sufficient expertise to diagnose their own ailments, pupils are often not best placed to make wise choices about their own learning, even if they *think* they are[3]. Misplaced autonomy can be worse than none at all.

Of course, there *are* some things we *can* give our pupils meaningful choice over without loss, such as what to focus an essay on or which formula to use in tackling a problem. Where these opportunities present themselves, we should embrace them.

However, in the vast majority of classroom cases, it is simply better for teachers to make an executive decision on behalf of pupils, and then work to boost *buy-in* for this choice[4].

Buy-in is a measure of how much someone actively supports a suggested course of action. It is generated by helping pupils understand *why* a decision is in their interests, and then providing opportunities for them to intentionally choose to go along with it. Let's call these strategies: *exposing the benefits* and *offering opt-in*.

The previous drivers operate at a predominantly unconscious level. *Boosting buy-in* involves elements of more conscious reasoning, and as we will see by the end by the chapter, even some *metacognition*.

Exposing the benefits

When pupils perceive and value the benefits of a decision, they are more likely to go along with it. This idea is obvious, but for several reasons, it is not something schools consistently carry out:

1. **Elusive returns** The value of what we teach is often nebulous and highly delayed. Articulating the benefits of *factorising quadratics* is tough, even for a teacher.
2. **Curse of knowledge** Because teachers know *so much* about their subjects, it can be easy to assume that the value of what we are teaching is simply *obvious*.
3. **Role resistance** *Salesperson* wasn't part of the job description. Peddling our subject – despite its importance – is not something our profession holds in high esteem.

Lesson time is precious. With the backdrop of these three reasons, taking time out to explain the *why* of our work can feel a luxury hard to justify.

However, exposing the benefits can take mere minutes, and the learning time recouped through elevated attention and effort can repay any initial outlay many times over. It's well worth the investment.

Exposing the benefits is about making deliberate decisions and then communicating the rationale behind them. It works best when we:

- **Frame** Emphasise the benefits from the perspective of our *pupils*, rather than why *we* or *society* might believe this opportunity is of value.
- **Expedite** Bring the benefits as *near* as possible[5]. Not just the value of this topic when you are 40, but next year, next week or even today. Of course, there is enormous value to learning in and of itself, but for many pupils, this can often be hard to sense *before* they have done it.
- **Moderate** Don't *overstate* the benefits. Not only is this ethically untenable, but it can have backfire effects on motivation, credibility and trust.

People differ in what they value, and so effective exposition relies not only on how well we know our *subject*, but how well we know our *pupils*. This is why empathy is such a cornerstone of teaching.

As well as thinking carefully about how we *construct* our pitch, we can also be intentional in how we *deliver* it. To help your message land well:

- **Overcommunicate** The more prominent a message is, the more likely we will refer to it when facing a choice. Spread your explanation over time and space[6].
- **Exemplify** The more tangible the picture we paint of the benefits, the stronger our impression of them. *Make it vivid* and *keep it real*.
- **Simplify** The easier and faster we process a message, the more we tend to value it. Make your message simple, clear and obvious.

Understanding the benefits is important but insufficient. To fully secure buy-in, we must also provide opportunities for pupils to actively *opt in* to a decision.

Offering opt-in

Offering *opt-in* is about creating the space for pupils to consider your selected course of action, and then actively *choose* to go along with it.

In the majority of scenarios, offering opt-in should be as lightweight as possible, and only deployed at critical points in the lesson sequence.

After explaining the why, we might simply provide pupils with a clear and simple next step and then ask: *Are you up for it?* or *Shall we crack on?* This micro-choice can make all the difference.

For situations where we *really* need to turn the dial on motivation, opt-in can be intensified by using some or all of the following:

- **Rationale elaboration** Getting pupils to summarise the 'why' in their own words and explore how it links to their personal goals or values[7].

- **Implementation intentions** Getting pupils to detail the steps they will take to be successful, including the where and when of their actions, plus how they will overcome any barriers that crop up along the way[8].
- **Commitment contracts** Getting pupils to publicly declare their endorsement and intentions, either verbally or on paper.

Of course, we need to be confident that pupils will respond positively to our offer. But if we've done a good job of *exposing the benefits*, and have a *trusting relationship*, then our pupils will be in the best position possible to make a *wise choice*.

The degree of buy-in we can generate is limited in part by the depth of understanding our pupils have about how motivation works. For example, knowing that *declarations of commitment can help people achieve their goals* makes it much more likely that pupils will go along with this activity.

For the highest levels of buy-in, we need to develop pupil *metamotivation*.

Metamotivation

Metamotivation is the ability to monitor and regulate our own motivation[9].

When pupils have high levels of metamotivation, they are likely to invest more attention in the opportunities we offer and sustain their effort with less support, both within and beyond the classroom. It is an effective instrument for independent learning.

We can develop metamotivation by teaching our pupils the ideas covered in this book (along with those in my previous book: *Memorable Teaching*) and helping them translate and apply them to the situations they face as learners.

Metamotivation is best taught *within* existing lessons, rather than as a standalone subject. And to do it well will require time, planning, and the co-ordination of multiple teachers over a pupil's school career. Even with this in place, it is likely we will only begin to scratch the surface.

However, this is an investment worth making. Just imagine how your pupils would approach their homework or prepare for exams if they had even higher levels of metamotivation. And perhaps more importantly: how they would steer their remaining years on earth.

Because fostering metamotivation isn't just about helping your pupils to learn more. It's also about growing their *agency* – their capacity to *act in the world* and *achieve their goals*. Which is why, alongside powerful curriculum knowledge, it's one of the greatest gifts we can give our pupils.

And that, folks, is the last of the 5 core drivers. You now have a suite of tools you can use to boost motivation for learning in the classroom. Let's finish by pulling them all together.

Summary of core strategies

- Expose the benefits of the choices you make for your pupils
- Provide opportunities for them to opt in
- Invest in building metamotivation

Notes & further reading

1. For more, see *When choice motivates and when it does not* by Katz bit.ly/mot-kat
2. For more on the benefits of meaningful choice, see *Increasing situational interest in the classroom* by Schraw bit.ly/mot-sch
3. For a helpful overview of this argument, see *When is student choice a good idea?* by Christodoulou bit.ly/mot-chr and *Dunning-Kruger: the gap between prediction and performance* by Read rsc.li/mot-rea
4. For more on influencing decisions, see *Choice architecture* by Thaler bit.ly/mot-tha
5. For more, see *Behavioural economics of education* by Lavecchia bit.ly/mot-lav
6. This is known as the 'Mere Exposure Effect'. For more, see bit.ly/mot-exp
7. For more, see *Behavioural insights for education* by O'Reilly bit.ly/mot-ore
8. For more, see *Implementation intentions to encourage student action* by Fletcher-Wood bit.ly/mot-fle2
9. For more, see *Metacognition and self-regulation* by EEF bit.ly/mot-eef and *New Directions in Self-Regulation: The Role of Metamotivational Beliefs* by Scholer bit.ly/mot-sch2

Pulling it all together

> "When we add up all those inches, that's gonna make the f*cking difference between winning and losing."
> Pacino

We've covered a lot: 9 *key ideas* to help us think productively about motivation and 5 *core drivers* to help us influence it.

Now it's time to pull all these elements together, so you get a sense of the *motivation for learning* framework as a whole. To achieve this, we'll:

1. Put *all* the elements together on one double-page spread.
2. Explore an *example* and a *non-example* of the framework in action.
3. Think about the framework and *you*.

And then to finish off, we'll explore one final *key idea*. But first, the framework in full:

Key ideas
1   Motivation influences behaviour, learning and wellbeing
2   It is complex and invisible which makes it hard to understand
3   To influence it, we must draw on insights from science
4   Motivation is a system for allocating attention
5   It allocates attention based on the best available investment
6   This is a largely unconscious process
7   And a specific response to the situation, not a general trait
8   *Motivation for learning* is something we must actively build
9   We can systematically build it by applying the 5 core drivers →
10   Motivation is an upstream cause of behaviour

The *motivation for learning* framework

Core drivers

Secure success	Give pupils a high success rate to look back on; frame what success means and help them attribute it accurately; pre-empt failure
Run routines	Make the *process* of learning easy, whilst keeping the *content* of learning challenging; script chains and cues; stick with it
Nudge norms	Elevate the visibility of desirable norms; amplify peer approval; emphasise what you *want* to happen, not what you *don't*
Build belonging	Signal the status of *all* pupils in your class; develop a unifying purpose and identify common ground; earn and keep trust
Boost buy-in	Expose the benefits of the choices you make for your pupils; provide opportunities for them to opt in; invest in building metamotivation

Download at **pepsmccrea.com/motivation**

Nora & Evie

To get a sense of the contrast the drivers can create, let's imagine two pupils, in different classrooms. Nora's teacher doesn't employ the drivers. Evie's teacher applies them liberally. In each situation, consider how much *attention* and *effort* each pupil is likely to invest in their learning:

- **Nora:** *"Science is duff. I'm always getting it wrong and the teacher is constantly chastising me, in front of everyone else. I shouldn't be so bothered because the rest of the class don't really care. They don't include me in their jokes and they're not interested in learning anyway. Miss Nelly is constantly telling us all how 'no-one ever does any homework'. Still, it's humiliating to be made to feel stupid. And there doesn't seem to be anything I can do about it. When I put my hand up, I get sneered at by other pupils, and I'm not even sure if Miss knows I exist. She sometimes calls me Dora [sad face]. I don't even correct her because who knows how she will react. I reckon I'm probably just not a 'science person'. Which is no big deal, because there doesn't seem to be any point in learning it anyway."*

- **Evie:** *"Science is hard, but I know how to get better. I know what to expect in lessons, and slowly but surely, I'm improving all the time. Even when I get it wrong, it's not a bad thing. Miss Elle quietly supports me, or we decide to share my experience with the rest of the class so everyone can learn from it. Our class is 'rooting to learn loads' and so I feel proud to contribute. It's a nice class to be in. We all 'get' and 'look out for' each other. And we try hard. Miss is always pointing out when someone is 'being an effective learner', and everyone always seems to do their homework. Miss Elle really wants me to do well. She knows the kind of things I struggle with and checks that I can see properly when we do demonstrations, every single time! Science is pretty cool. Without it, I wouldn't have my glasses or be able to play Minecraft. It's a worthwhile lesson to have."*

Of course, these are two ends of a spectrum and individual differences have an influence, but still: these examples give us a sense of just how much of a difference the core drivers can make. Not only to pupils, but also to their teachers: imagine being Miss Nelly or Miss Elle.

Now let's pause and consider your *own* approach:

1. Flick back a few pages to the framework overview.
2. Choose one class and think about how intentionally you are activating each driver.
3. List out the things you could do to build *even greater* motivation for learning.
4. And then pick one small thing to *plan for* and *try out* next time you are teaching.

Don't let yourself skip this bit – it will only take a few minutes and will make all the difference in the long run. Flick back and then fill in the radar*:

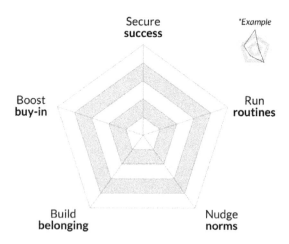

Ways you could build *even greater* motivation for learning in your lessons:

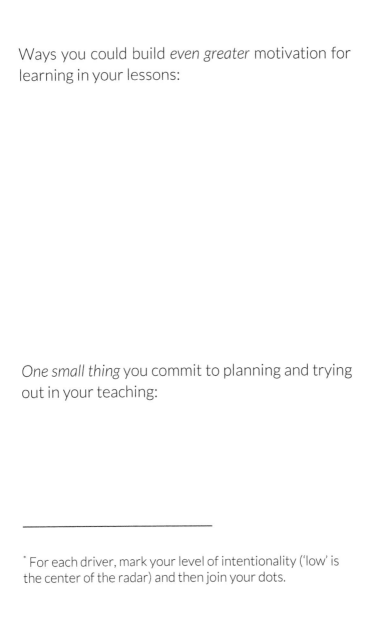

One small thing you commit to planning and trying out in your teaching:

---

* For each driver, mark your level of intentionality ('low' is the center of the radar) and then join your dots.

Upstream thinking

One of the things that makes motivation so interesting is its relationship with *behaviour*.

Motivation is an *upstream cause* of behaviour[1]. This is important, because the further upstream we intervene, the more leverage we have over any outcomes[2].

Just as healthcare systems save more lives when they focus on *helping people quit smoking* as well as *improving cancer treatment*, and fire services reduce casualties when they *invest in fitting smoke alarms* alongside *improving fire truck response times*, schools can be more effective when they aim to *influence behaviour before it happens* as well as *addressing it after it has occurred*[3].

However, achieving this takes planning and resolve. The sheer *visibility* and *immediacy* of behaviour means that, in the busy environment of the classroom, the work of building motivation can easily get pushed to one side.

When we let this happen, when schools focus on behaviour at the expense of motivation, they can quickly find themselves drawn towards a culture of *superficial compliance*, of being satisfied with suppressing bad behaviour, keeping pupils in the room, and ensuring that 'the work gets done'.

But when we find the resolve and do the planning, when schools get the balance between behaviour and motivation *right*, schools can find themselves leaning towards a culture of *deep commitment*, of being satisfied only when pupils care lots about their learning, put in mountains of effort, and sustain this even when the 'going gets tough' which, I'm sure you'll agree, is a balance worth striving for.

Key idea *Motivation is an upstream cause of behaviour*

And that's it folks: the framework in full and how we can use it to serve our pupils. But before we sign off, let's do one last thing: let's explore how we might harness the framework to serve our *selves*.

Notes & further reading

1. Motivation is perhaps best thought of as 'behavioural (or attentional) potential'. From this perspective, when motivation meets opportunity, we get behaviour. *Motivation + Opportunity = Behaviour*. The activation of this equation can sometimes also require a 'prompt' > for a helpful model that includes a prompt component, see *Tiny Habits* by Fogg bit.ly/mot-fog
2. For a full account of this idea, see *Upstream: the quest to solve problems before they happen* by Heath
3. This is what Bennett calls 'Getting in front of the behaviour' in *Running the room*. For further proactive strategies, see *Reducing behaviour problems in the elementary school classroom* by IES bit.ly/mot-ies

Motivating ourselves

> "Success is a science – if you have the conditions, you get the results."
> Oscar Wilde

We've talked a lot about motivating our pupils. But what about motivating ourselves? Are we any different? Do we need help to achieve our goals, or can we just rely on *willpower*?

Whilst we certainly *can* bring willpower to bear, lapses in self-regulation are a standard feature of life for all but the most self-disciplined adult[1].

This is perfectly normal. Whether it's *eating that biscuit* or watching just *one more episode*, most people struggle to act in their own best interests in some way or other, particularly when we're faced with more immediately satisfying options.

One reason behind this is our poor ability to forecast how we will feel in the future[2].

We consistently anticipate that we'll make *better decisions tomorrow*, despite *continually crumbling today*. This false optimism persists even when we begin to notice it in others.

The situation is compounded by our tendency to retrofit narratives to explain our past action[3]. No matter how tenuous, we nearly always have a reason for our responses, which only makes it even harder to recognise and learn from poor prior decisions.

The challenge of self-regulation is ever more prescient given the increasing abundance of immediately satisfying options in modern life.

From *chocolate by the check-out* to *video-on-demand*, these temptations can easily trigger failures in self-regulation and in doing so, deprive us of achieving important life goals and even direct us towards a variety of health ailments[4].

So, what can we do beyond applying willpower? How can we better manage our motivation in the moment?

One option is to practise *mindfulness*[5]. This can help us build a stronger awareness and influence over our attention and emotional state.

Another approach is to *reframe* our decisions. When faced with a choice in the present, we can ask ourselves what we would do in the future: *if I was faced with this option next week, how would I respond?*

Mindfulness and reframing can be powerful approaches, but they take time and ongoing practice. And they can often come apart in times of stress, which is when we need them the most.

For the busy professional, we need something that can deliver reliable results without taking loads of time. We need *motivational architecture*.

Motivational architecture

Motivational architecture is about recognising the power of our unconscious and modifying our environment to get it working *for us*, not *against us*.

Whilst we might not be able to beat our unconscious in the moment, we *can* outsmart it with some advance notice. Deleting twitter from your phone or putting your alarm at the far side of the room is about planning, not willpower[6].

To begin, we can simply use the ideas and strategies from this book. The 5 drivers work just as well for our *selves* as they do for our *pupils*.

To illustrate *how*, let's consider a scenario. Imagine you wanted to get better at motivating your pupils. You have the knowledge, now you just need to make the change. What can you do?

On the next page is an example of the kinds of strategies we might consider if we thought about this problem through the lens of the 5 drivers[7]:

	Core drivers
Secure success	Start with one tiny, achievable change and ramp up gradually; define success, track your progress and plan for failure; the more you succeed, the more you will *want* to do it again
Run routines	Choose a change you can practise daily; replace a routine, don't add; design a cue you can't miss, make it easy to get started and then 'show up' consistently to ingrain the habit
Nudge norms	Surround yourself with people who are doing the same thing and are passionate about it; in real life or virtually; join a club or just set one up
Build belonging	Get to know others doing similar things and share your own experiences; align your work around a purpose and assign yourself a title or identity (eg 'research geek')
Boost buy-in	Carve out regular opportunities to clarify *why* you are doing this; publicly declare your intentions and commit to doing a course, or even just a blog or school presentation

Now choose something *you* want to get better at and try it out for yourself:

Core drivers	
Secure success	
Run routines	
Nudge norms	
Build belonging	
Boost buy-in	

Envisage using the above approach to secure your *New Year's resolutions* rather than relying on willpower. Imagine the difference in results.

Not only is this an efficient way to achieve your goals, but it can also slash the need for ongoing self-regulation and so free us up to *focus more on the moment*.

Motivational architecture enables us to live with both more intention *and* attention. Which is why for me, it's the *ultimate human superpower*.

And with that grand claim, we draw to a close. It's been a blast. From the mechanics of motivation to the design of our dreams, we've covered a lot.

But this is only a *start*. The big picture has been sketched, but the details are yet to be crafted. And the baton has now been passed to *you*.

Translate these ideas for your classroom, read up on what piques your interest, and share generously what you learn. Let's move the profession onwards one shared insight at a time.

I'm *enormously* grateful that you've chosen to invest your precious time in exploring these ideas and approaches with me and I hope that some of it sticks as you make your way through the world. And if our paths should cross, do stop, say hi and tell me what you think[8].

Now go motivate.

Notes & further reading

1. For a cracking overview of this situation, see *Beyond Willpower: Strategies for reducing failures of self-control* by Duckworth bit.ly/mot-duc
2. For more, see the *Choiceology podcast: ep. 7* with Milkman bit.ly/mot-mil
3. For some mind-blowing insight on just how far this concept goes, see *The mind is flat* by Chater bit.ly/mot-cha
4. For more on the potential benefits and detriments, see *New directions in self-regulation: the role of metamotivation* by Scholer bit.ly/mot-sch2

5. **Note** Practising mindfulness can have both positive and negative outcomes. For effects on pupils, see this systematic review by Campbell Collaboration bit.ly/mot-cam and for effects on adults, see this mixed-methods study by Clarke bit.ly/mot-cla > if, after considering all this, you do want to have a play, a great place to start is the Headspace.com app which, at the time of publication is free for teachers headspace.com/educators
6. For more, see *Why willpower is overrated* by Resnick bit.ly/mot-res
7. For a deep dive into habit formation (which has lots of overlap with motivational architecture), see *Atomic habits* by Clear
8. The most likely place to find me is at a ResearchED or similar UK education conference. However, you don't have to wait for a face-to-face encounter to tell me what you think: just ping me an email at pepsmccrea@gmail.com or message me on twitter at @PepsMccrea

Thank yous

Writing doesn't happen in a vacuum. To everyone who contributed in some way or other during the 3-year epic journey to make this book happen, *thank you*. Special snaps to:

- Mum & Dad, again, for proofreading, encouragement and bottomless childcare!
- Karlos, again, for relentlessly enduring the search for truth over many hilly miles.
- Marie, Matt and everyone else who set and hold the bar high for our sector.
- Tom, Helene and the ResearchED community for fanning the flames.
- To Nick, who triggered a lastminute 6-month re-write which, after 2.5 years, was *painful*, but absolutely the right thing to do.
- And to Alasdair, Bréanainn, Caroline, Cecil, Dave, David, Hari, Helene, Jacynth, Jen, Jo, Josh, Julian, Lawrence, Mike and all you other legends who have weighed in to help make this book the best it can be.

Collect 'em all...

Praise for the *High Impact Teaching* series:

"If you have a spare half-hour or so, you could read *Memorable Teaching* from cover to cover. I doubt you'll find an education book with more useful insights per minute of reading time."
Dylan Wiliam, Emeritus Professor of Educational Assessment at UCL

"How to improve your teaching by planning better. Things that make teachers' lives simpler like that are few and far between."
Doug Lemov, Author of Teach Like a Champion

Notes

Printed in the USA
CPSIA information can be obtained
at www.ICGtesting.com
LVHW010047191223
766854LV00054BA/1981